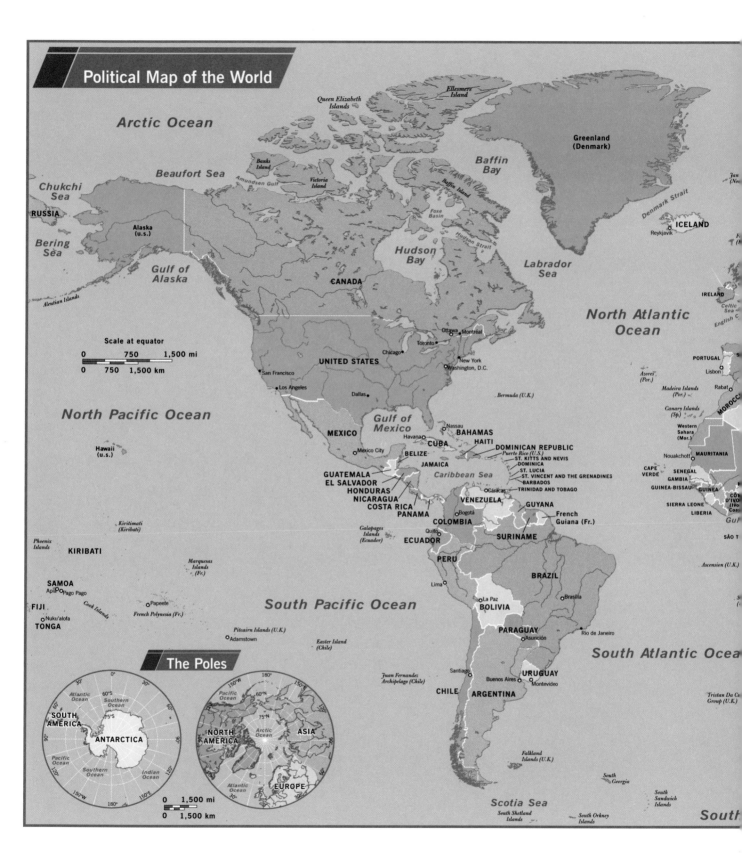

Political Map of the World

Arctic Ocean

Queen Elizabeth Islands

Ellesmere Island

Greenland (Denmark)

Baffin Bay

Banks Island

Beaufort Sea

Amundsen Gulf

Victoria Island

Baffin Island

Chukchi Sea

RUSSIA

Alaska (u.s.)

Bering Sea

Gulf of Alaska

Aleutian Islands

Denmark Strait

ICELAND
Reykjavik

Fox Basin

Hudson Strait

Hudson Bay

Labrador Sea

CANADA

IRELAND

Celtic Sea

North Atlantic Ocean

English C.

Ottawa Montréal
Toronto

Chicago

New York
Washington, D.C.

UNITED STATES

San Francisco

North Pacific Ocean

Los Angeles

Dallas

Bermuda (U.K.)

PORTUGAL
Lisbon

Azores (Por.)

Madeira Islands (Por.)

Rabat
MOROCCO

MEXICO

Gulf of Mexico

Mexico City

Nassau

BAHAMAS

Havana
CUBA

HAITI

DOMINICAN REPUBLIC

Puerto Rico (U.S.)
ST. KITTS AND NEVIS
DOMINICA

Canary Islands (Sp.)

Western Sahara (Mor.)

Nouakchott

MAURITANIA

Hawaii (u.s.)

BELIZE

JAMAICA

GUATEMALA
EL SALVADOR
HONDURAS
NICARAGUA
COSTA RICA
PANAMA

Caribbean Sea

ST. LUCIA
ST. VINCENT AND THE GRENADINES
BARBADOS
TRINIDAD AND TOBAGO

Caracas

VENEZUELA

GUYANA

French Guiana (Fr.)

COLOMBIA

Bogotá

CAPE VERDE

SENEGAL
GAMBIA
GUINEA-BISSAU

GUINEA

SIERRA LEONE

LIBERIA

CÔTE D'IVO
(Ivo. Coas

Kiritimati (Kiribati)

Galapagos Islands (Ecuador)

Quito

ECUADOR

SURINAME

Gul

SÃO T

Phoenix Islands

KIRIBATI

Marquesas Islands (Fr.)

PERU

Lima

BRAZIL

Ascension (U.K.)

SAMOA

Apia Pago Pago

FIJI

Nuku'alofa

TONGA

Cook Islands

Papeete

French Polynesia (Fr.)

South Pacific Ocean

La Paz
BOLIVIA

Brasília

S
(

Pitcairn Islands (U.K.)

Adamstown

Easter Island (Chile)

PARAGUAY

Asunción

Rio de Janeiro

South Atlantic Ocea

Juan Fernandez Archipelago (Chile)

Santiago

Buenos Aires

URUGUAY

Montevideo

Tristan Da Cu Group (U.K.)

CHILE

ARGENTINA

Falkland Islands (U.K.)

South Georgia

The Poles

30° *0°* *30°*
Atlantic Ocean *60°S* *Southern Ocean*
75°S

SOUTH AMERICA

ANTARCTICA

Pacific Ocean *Southern Ocean* *Indian Ocean*

60°W *120°E*

150°W *180°* *150°E*

180° *150°W*
Pacific Ocean *150°E*
60°N

75°N *Arctic Ocean*

ASIA

NORTH AMERICA

Atlantic Ocean *30°*

EUROPE

0   1,500 mi
0   1,500 km

Scale at equator

0   750   1,500 mi
0   750   1,500 km

Scotia Sea

South Shetland Islands

South Orkney Islands

South Sandwich Islands

South

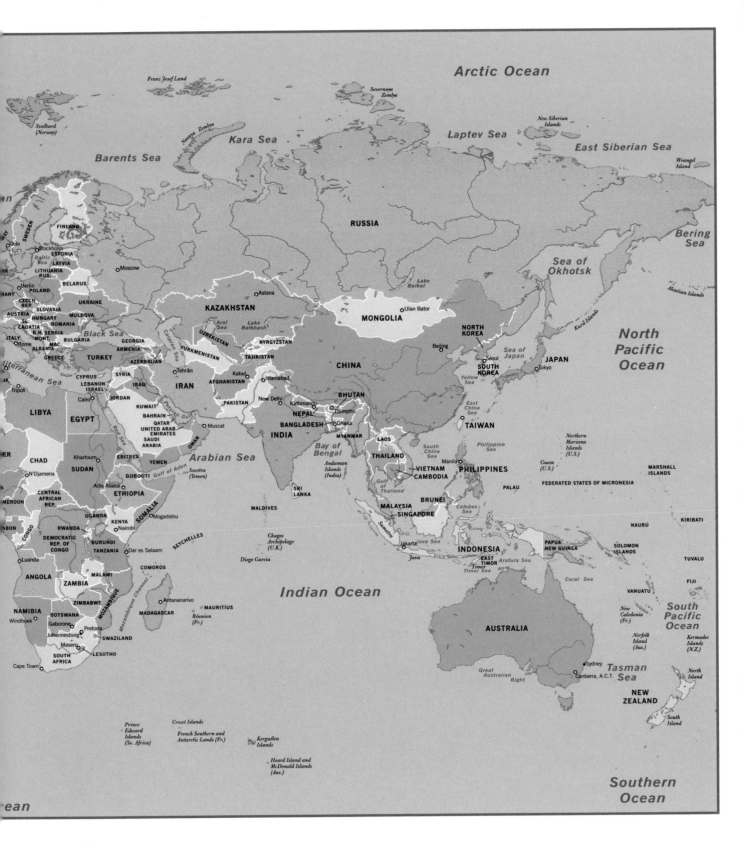

SEVENTH TEXAS EDITION

We the People

AN INTRODUCTION TO AMERICAN POLITICS

SEVENTH TEXAS EDITION

We the People

AN INTRODUCTION TO AMERICAN POLITICS

Benjamin Ginsberg
THE JOHNS HOPKINS UNIVERSITY

Theodore J. Lowi
CORNELL UNIVERSITY

Margaret Weir
UNIVERSITY OF CALIFORNIA AT BERKELEY

Anthony Champagne
UNIVERSITY OF TEXAS AT DALLAS

Edward J. Harpham
UNIVERSITY OF TEXAS AT DALLAS

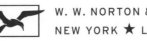

W. W. NORTON & COMPANY
NEW YORK ★ LONDON

W. W. Norton & Company has been independent since its founding in 1923, when William Warder Norton and Mary D. Herter Norton first published lectures delivered at the People's Institute, the adult education division of New York City's Cooper Union. The Nortons soon expanded their program beyond the Institute, publishing books by celebrated academics from America and abroad. By mid-century, the two major pillars of Norton's publishing program—trade books and college texts—were firmly established. In the 1950s, the Norton family transferred control of the company to its employees, and today—with a staff of four hundred and a comparable number of trade, college, and professional titles published each year—W. W. Norton & Company stands as the largest and oldest publishing house owned wholly by its employees.

Editor: Ann Shin
Editorial assistant: Mollie Eisenberg
Project editor: Carla L. Talmadge
Senior production manager, College: Ben Reynolds
Book design: Rubina Yeh and Joan Greenfield
Figures: John McAusland
Managing editor, College: Marian Johnson
Composition: TSI Graphics
Manufacturing: R. R. Donnelley & Sons—Willard Division
Cover design: Joan Greenfield
Cover illustration: Mick Wiggins
Photo editor: Kelly Mitchell
Photo research: Patty Cateura, Elyse Rieder, and Rae Grant
E-media editor: Dan Jost

Library of Congress Cataloging-in-Publication Data

We the people : an introduction to American politics / Benjamin Ginsberg ...
[et al.].—7th Texas ed.
       p. cm.
Includes bibliographical references and index.

ISBN 978-0-393-93239-3 (hardcover)

1. United States—Politics and government—Textbooks. 2. Texas—Politics and government—Textbooks. I. Ginsberg, Benjamin.

JK276.W4 2009
320.473—dc22   2008049970

W. W. Norton & Company, Inc., 500 Fifth Avenue, New York, N.Y. 10110
www.wwnorton.com

W. W. Norton & Company Ltd., Castle House, 75/76 Wells Street, London W1T 3QT

1 2 3 4 5 6 7 8 9 0

TO

SANDY, CINDY, AND ALEX GINSBERG

ANGELE, ANNA, AND JASON LOWI

NICHOLAS ZIEGLER

CONTENTS

PREFACE *xxv*

ACKNOWLEDGMENTS *xxvii*

PART I | Foundations

1 ★ American Political Culture   2

What Americans Think about Government   5
Trust in Government   7
Political Efficacy   9
Citizenship: Knowledge and Participation   10
The Necessity of Political Knowledge   11
Government   14
Is Government Needed?   14
Forms of Government   14
Limiting Government   15
Access to Government: The Expansion of Participation   16
Influencing the Government through Participation: Politics   16
Who Are Americans?   18
Immigration and Ethnic Diversity   20
Immigration and Race   21
Twenty-First-Century Americans   22
Thinking Critically about American Political Culture   26
Liberty   26
Equality   28
Democracy   28
Does the System Uphold American Political Values? Thinking Critically about
    Liberty, Equality, and Democracy   29
Who Benefits from Government?   35
For Further Reading   36
Recommended Web Sites   36
Study Outline   37
Practice Quiz   38
Key Terms   39

2 ★ The Founding and the Constitution   40

The First Founding: Interests and Conflicts   43
British Taxes and Colonial Interests   43

Political Strife and the Radicalizing of the Colonists 44

The Declaration of Independence 45

The Articles of Confederation 46

The Second Founding: From Compromise to Constitution 47

International Standing and Balance of Power 47

The Annapolis Convention 47

Shays's Rebellion 48

The Constitutional Convention 48

The Constitution 53

The Legislative Branch 53

The Executive Branch 55

The Judicial Branch 56

National Unity and Power 56

Amending the Constitution 57

Ratifying the Constitution 57

Constitutional Limits on the National Government's Power 57

The Fight for Ratification 60

Federalists versus Antifederalists 61

Reflections on the Founding 64

The Citizen's Role and the Changing Constitution 66

Amendments: Many Are Called, Few Are Chosen 66

The Case of the Equal Rights Amendment 67

Which Were Chosen? An Analysis of the Twenty-Seven 70

The Supreme Court and Constitutional Amendment 72

Thinking Critically about Liberty, Equality, and Democracy 73

For Further Reading 76

Recommended Web Sites 76

Study Outline 77

Practice Quiz 78

Key Terms 79

3 ★ Federalism 80

The Federal Framework 83

Federalism in the Constitution 83

Restraining National Power with Dual Federalism, 1789–1937 88

Federalism and the Slow Growth of the National Government's Power 91

The Changing Role of the States 92

Who Does What? The Changing Federal Framework 96

Expansion of the National Government 96

Federal Grants 97

Cooperative Federalism 98

Regulated Federalism and National Standards 99

New Federalism and State Control 103

Devolution: For Whose Benefit? 107

Federalism since 2000 109

**Thinking Critically about Liberty versus Equality in the
Federal System 111**

For Further Reading 114

Recommended Web Sites 114

Study Outline *115*
Practice Quiz *115*
Key Terms *116*

4 ★ Civil Liberties *118*

A Brief History of the Bill of Rights *121*
Nationalizing the Bill of Rights *121*
The First Amendment and Freedom of Religion *125*
Separation between Church and State *125*
Free Exercise of Religion *127*
The First Amendment and Freedom of Speech and the Press *128*
Freedom of the Press *133*
The Second Amendment and the Right to Bear Arms *138*
Due Process of Law *139*
The Fourth Amendment and Searches and Seizures *140*
The Fifth Amendment *142*
The Sixth Amendment and the Right to Counsel *144*
The Eighth Amendment and Cruel and Unusual Punishment *146*
The Right to Privacy *147*
Thinking Critically about the Future of Civil Liberties *152*
For Further Reading *153*
Recommended Web Sites *153*
Study Outline *154*
Practice Quiz *155*
Key Terms *155*

5 ★ Civil Rights *156*

The Struggle for Civil Rights *159*
Slavery and the Abolitionist Movement *159*
The Link to the Women's Rights Movement *160*
The Civil War Amendments to the Constitution *161*
Civil Rights and the Supreme Court: "Separate but Equal" *163*
Organizing for Equality *163*
Litigating for Equality after World War II *165*
Civil Rights after *Brown v. Board of Education* *167*
The Civil Rights Acts *171*
The Universalization of Civil Rights *177*
Women and Gender Discrimination *178*
Latinos *182*
Asian Americans *184*
Native Americans *186*
Disabled Americans *187*
The Aged *188*
Gays and Lesbians *188*
Affirmative Action *191*
The Supreme Court and the Burden of Proof *192*
Referenda on Affirmative Action *195*
Thinking Critically about the Affirmative Action Debate *196*

For Further Reading *199*
Recommended Web Sites *199*
Study Outline *200*
Practice Quiz *201*
Key Terms *201*

PART II Politics

6 ★ Public Opinion 204

Understanding Public Opinion **207**
Political Values *207*
Forms of Disagreement *209*
How Political Values Are Formed *209*
Influences on Our Political Values *210*
From Political Values to Ideology *218*
How We Form Political Opinions **221**
Political Knowledge *224*
The Influence of Political Leaders, Private Groups, and the Media *226*
Measuring Public Opinion **231**
Constructing Public Opinion from Surveys *231*
Thinking Critically about Public Opinion and Democracy **239**
For Further Reading **242**
Recommended Web Sites **242**
Study Outline **243**
Practice Quiz **244**
Key Terms **244**

7 ★ The Media 246

The Media Industry and Government **249**
Types of Media *249*
Regulation of the Broadcast Media *254*
Organization and Ownership of the Media *255*
Nationalization of the News *258*
News Coverage **259**
Journalists *259*
Subjects of the News *261*
The Power of Consumers *264*
Media Power in American Politics **266**
Shaping Events *266*
The Sources of Media Power *267*
The Rise of Adversarial Journalism *272*
Thinking Critically about Media Power and Democracy **276**
The Power of the New Media *277*
For Further Reading **278**
Recommended Web Sites **278**

Study Outline *279*
Practice Quiz *280*
Key Terms *281*

8 ★ Political Participation and Voting *282*

Forms of Political Participation *285*
Voting *288*
Who Participates, and How? *291*
African Americans *293*
Latinos *296*
Asian Americans *296*
Women versus Men *298*
Religious Identity and Politics *299*
Age and Participation *301*
Explaining Political Participation *303*
Socioeconomic Status *303*
Civic Engagement *305*
Formal Obstacles *306*
Political Mobilization *309*
Thinking Critically about Political Participation and Liberty, Equality, and Democracy *314*
For Further Reading *315*
Recommended Web Sites *316*
Study Outline *316*
Practice Quiz *317*
Key Terms *317*

9 ★ Political Parties *318*

What Are Political Parties? *321*
The Two-Party System in America *322*
Historical Origins *322*
Party Systems *325*
Electoral Alignments and Realignments *330*
American Third Parties *332*
Party Organization *335*
National Convention *335*
National Committee *338*
Congressional Campaign Committees *340*
State and Local Party Organizations *340*
Parties and the Electorate *341*
Group Affiliations *343*
Parties and Elections *346*
Recruiting Candidates *346*
Nominations *346*
Getting Out the Vote *348*
Facilitating Voter Choice *348*

Parties and Government *349*
Parties and Policy *349*
Parties in Congress *350*
President and Party *352*
Thinking Critically about the Role of Parties in a Democracy *354*
For Further Reading *359*
Recommended Web Sites *359*
Study Outline *360*
Practice Quiz *361*
Key Terms *361*

10 ★ Campaigns and Elections *362*

Elections in America *365*
Types of Elections *365*
The Criteria for Winning *366*
Electoral Districts *367*
The Ballot *369*
The Electoral College *371*
Election Campaigns *373*
Advisers *373*
Polling *374*
The Primaries *376*
Presidential Elections *377*
The Convention *379*
The General Election Campaign and High-Tech Politics *382*
Campaigns and Political Equality: From Labor-Intensive to Capital-Intensive
    Politics *388*
How Voters Decide *389*
Partisan Loyalty *389*
Issues *390*
Candidate Characteristics *392*
The 2008 Election *393*
The Path to 2008: Modern Electoral Politics and Race *394*
The 2008 Campaigns *398*
Money and Politics *405*
Sources of Campaign Funds *405*
Implications for Democracy *410*
Thinking Critically about the Electoral Process *412*
For Further Reading *412*
Recommended Web Sites *413*
Study Outline *414*
Practice Quiz *415*
Key Terms *415*

11 ★ Groups and Interests 416

The Character of Interest Groups 419
What Interests Are Represented? 420
What Interests Are Not Represented? 423
Organizational Components 423
The Characteristics of Members 427
The Proliferation of Groups 428
The Expansion of Government 428
The New Politics Movement and Public Interest Groups 429
Strategies: The Quest for Political Power 430
Direct Lobbying 431
Cultivating Access 434
Using the Courts (Litigation) 437
Mobilizing Public Opinion 438
Using Electoral Politics 440
**Thinking Critically about Groups and Interests: The Dilemmas of
     Reform 447**
For Further Reading 449
Recommended Web Sites 449
Study Outline 450
Practice Quiz 451
Key Terms 451

PART III / Institutions

12 ★ Congress 454

Congress: Representing the American People 457
House and Senate: Differences in Representation 457
Sociological versus Agency Representation 458
The Electoral Connection 461
Direct Patronage 466
The Organization of Congress 468
Party Leadership in the House 468
Party Leadership in the Senate 469
The Committee System 471
The Staff System: Staffers and Agencies 475
Informal Organization: The Caucuses 476
Rules of Lawmaking: How a Bill Becomes a Law 476
Committee Deliberation 476
Debate 478
Conference Committee: Reconciling House and Senate Versions of
     Legislation 480
Presidential Action 482
How Congress Decides 482
Constituency 482
Interest Groups 483

Party Discipline   *484*
Weighing Diverse Influences   *490*
Beyond Legislation: Other Congressional Powers   491
Oversight   *491*
Advice and Consent: Special Senate Powers   *493*
Impeachment   *494*
Thinking Critically about Congress and Democracy   495
For Further Reading   498
Recommended Web Sites   498
Study Outline   499
Practice Quiz   500
Key Terms   501

13 ★ The Presidency   502

The Constitutional Basis of the Presidency   505
The Constitutional Powers of the Presidency   506
Expressed Powers   *508*
Delegated Powers   *517*
The Presidency as an Institution   520
The Cabinet   *520*
The White House Staff   *522*
The Executive Office of the President   *522*
The Vice Presidency   *523*
The First Spouse   *525*
The President and Policy   *525*
The Contemporary Bases of Presidential Power   526
Party as a Source of Power   *527*
Going Public   *527*
The Administrative State   *530*
Thinking Critically about Presidential Power and Democracy   536
For Further Reading   539
Recommended Web Sites   539
Study Outline   540
Practice Quiz   541
Key Terms   542

14 ★ Bureaucracy in a Democracy   544

Bureaucracy and Bureaucrats   547
The Size of the Federal Service   *547*
Bureaucrats   *549*
The Organization of the Executive Branch   552
Promoting the Public Welfare   *554*
Providing National Security   *557*
Maintaining a Strong Economy   *565*
Can Bureaucracy Be Reinvented?   569
Can the Bureaucracy Be Reduced?   571
Termination   *571*
Devolution   *572*

Privatization *574*
Can Bureaucracy Be Controlled? **577**
The President as Chief Executive *577*
Thinking Critically about Responsible Bureaucracy in a Democracy **580**
For Further Reading **584**
Recommended Web Sites **584**
Study Outline **585**
Practice Quiz **585**
Key Terms **586**

15 ★ The Federal Courts 588

The Legal System **591**
Cases and the Law *591*
Types of Courts *592*
Federal Jurisdiction **595**
Federal Trial Courts *595*
Federal Appellate Courts *596*
The Supreme Court *596*
How Judges Are Appointed *597*
The Power of the Supreme Court: Judicial Review **601**
Judicial Review of Acts of Congress *601*
Judicial Review of State Actions *601*
Judicial Review of Federal Agency Actions *602*
Judicial Review and Presidential Power *603*
Judicial Review and Lawmaking *604*
The Supreme Court in Action *607*
Controlling the Flow of Cases *609*
Lobbying for Access: Interests and the Court *611*
The Supreme Court's Procedures *615*
Explaining Supreme Court Decisions *618*
Judicial Power and Politics **619**
Traditional Limitations on the Federal Courts *621*
Two Judicial Revolutions *622*
Thinking Critically about the Judiciary, Liberty, and Democracy **624**
For Further Reading **625**
Recommended Web Sites **625**
Study Outline **626**
Practice Quiz **627**
Key Terms **627**

PART IV Policy

16 ★ Government and the Economy 630

The Goals of Economic Policy **633**
Promoting Stable Markets *633*
Promoting Economic Prosperity *635*

Promoting Business Development *639*
Protecting Employees and Consumers *641*
Four Schools of Economic Thought *643*
The Tools of Economic Policy 645
Monetary Policies *645*
Fiscal Policies *648*
Regulation and Antitrust Policy *653*
Subsidies and Contracting *657*
The Environment and the Economy 659
The Debate on Global Warming *660*
Environmental Policies *661*
The Politics of Economic Policy Making 666
Thinking Critically about Economic Policy 670
For Further Reading 673
Recommended Web Sites 673
Study Outline 673
Practice Quiz 675
Key Terms 675

17 ★ Social Policy 676

The Welfare State 679
The History of the Social Welfare System *679*
Foundations of the Welfare State *681*
Welfare Reform *685*
How Do We Pay for the Welfare State? *687*
Opening Opportunity 691
Education Policies *691*
Employment and Training Programs *693*
Health Policies *694*
Housing Policies *699*
Who Gets What from Social Policy? 701
The Elderly *701*
The Middle Class *703*
The Working Poor *703*
The Nonworking Poor *704*
Minorities, Women, and Children *704*
Thinking Critically about Social Policy and Equality 707
For Further Reading 710
Recommended Web Sites 710
Study Outline 711
Practice Quiz 712
Key Terms 713

18 ★ Foreign Policy and Democracy 714

The Nature of Foreign Policy 716
The Goals of Foreign Policy 718
Security *718*
Economic Prosperity *721*

International Humanitarian Policies   *724*

Who Makes American Foreign Policy?   727

The President   *727*

The Bureaucracy   *728*

Congress   *729*

Interest Groups   *731*

The Media   *733*

Putting It Together   *734*

The Instruments of Modern American Foreign Policy   734

Diplomacy   *735*

The United Nations   *736*

The International Monetary Structure   *738*

Economic Aid and Sanctions   *740*

Collective Security   *740*

Military Force   *742*

Arbitration   *743*

Foreign Policy and America's Place in the World   744

Four Visions of America's Role in the World   *744*

Thinking Critically about America's Role in the World Today   746

The Cold War and the Holy Alliance Role   *746*

The Post–Cold War Era and Global Capitalism   *748*

The Holy Alliance or the Napoleonic Role in the Post–Cold War Era?   *749*

The War on Terror: From Holy Alliance to Napoleonic Unilateralism   *752*

For Further Reading   753

Recommended Web Sites   753

Study Outline   754

Practice Quiz   755

Key Terms   756

PART V Texas Politics

19 ★ The Political Culture, People, and Economy of Texas   758

Texas Political Culture   761

The One-Party State   *762*

Provincialism   *762*

Business Dominance   *763*

The Land   763

The Gulf Coastal Plains   *764*

The Interior Lowlands   *765*

The Great Plains   *765*

The Basin and Range Province   *765*

Economic Change in Texas   765

Cotton   *766*

Cattle Ranching   *767*

Oil in the Texas Economy   *768*

The Emergence of the High-Tech Economy   *772*

NAFTA *773*
The People: Texas Demography 775
Anglos *776*
Hispanics *777*
African Americans *778*
Age *781*
Poverty and Wealth *781*
Urbanization 782
The Urban Political Economy *783*
Conclusion: Liberty, Equality, and Democracy in Texas 786
Recommended Web Sites 788
Study Outline 789
Practice Quiz 789
Key Terms 790

20 ★ The Texas Constitution 792

The Role of a State Constitution 795
The First Texas Constitutions 796
The Constitution of Coahuila y Tejas, 1827 *797*
The Constitution of the Republic of Texas, 1836 *798*
The Texas State Constitution of 1845 *801*
The Constitution of 1861: Texas Joins the Confederacy *802*
The Constitution of 1866: Texas Rejoins the Union *803*
The Reconstruction Constitution of 1869 *804*
The Constitution of 1876 805
The Constitution of Texas Today 807
The Preamble *807*
Article I: Bill of Rights *808*
Article II: The Powers of Government *808*
Article III: Legislative Department *809*
Article IV: Executive Department *810*
Article V: Judicial Department *810*
Article VI: Suffrage *811*
Article VII: Education *811*
Article VIII: Taxation and Revenue *811*
Articles IX and XI: Local Government *812*
Articles X, XII, XIII, and XIV *812*
Article XV: Impeachment *812*
Article XVI: General Provisions *813*
Article XVII: Amending the Constitution *813*
Recent Attempts to Rewrite the Texas Constitution 814
Sharpstown and the Failed Constitutional Reforms of 1974 *814*
The 1999 Ratliff-Junell Proposal *815*
The 2007 Amendments *816*
Conclusion: Thinking Critically about the Texas Constitution 820
Recommended Web Sites 821
Study Outline 822
Practice Quiz 823
Key Terms 823

21 ★ Parties and Elections in Texas   824

The Role of Political Parties in Texas Politics   827
Party Organization   828
Texas's History as a One-Party State   829
The Growth of the Republican Party   831
Issues in Texas Party Politics   833
Running as an Independent   833
Party Unity and Disunity   835
Hispanics and the Future of Party Politics in Texas   835
Elections in Texas   838
Primary Elections   839
General Election   839
Special Elections   840
Participation in Texas Elections   841
Earlier Restrictions on the Franchise   841
Qualifications to Vote   844
Low Voter Turnout   844
Early Voting   846
Campaigns   847
Conclusion   851
Recommended Web Sites   852
Study Outline   852
Practice Quiz   853
Key Terms   854

22 ★ Interest Groups, Lobbying, and Lobbyists   856

Interest Groups in the Political Process   859
Interest Groups and Policy Makers   860
Types of Interest Groups and Lobbyists   862
Getting Access to Policy Makers   864
Who Represents Bubba?   866
Another Side to Lobbying   867
Getting Out the Vote   869
Defeating Opponents   870
Individuals as Lobbyists   872
Conclusion   873
Recommended Web Sites   874
Study Outline   874
Practice Quiz   875
Key Terms   875

23 ★ The Texas Legislature   876

Structure   879
Bicameralism   880
Membership   880

Sessions of the Legislature 882
Regular Sessions *882*
Special Sessions *882*
Powers of the Legislature 883
Legislative Powers *883*
Nonlegislative Powers *884*
How a Bill Becomes a Law in Texas 885
Introduction in the House *886*
Referral *886*
Committee Action *888*
Floor Action *888*
Conference Committee *888*
Governor *890*
Other Players in the Legislative Process 890
Governor *891*
Comptroller of Public Accounts *892*
Media *892*
Courts *892*
Lobbyists *892*
Public *893*
Power in the Legislature 893
Leadership *893*
Centralizing Power: Sources of the Leadership's Power *894*
Redistricting *897*
Power and Partisanship in the Redistricting Battle *898*
Conclusion: Democracy and the Texas State Legislature 901
Recommended Web Sites 901
Study Outline 902
Practice Quiz 903
Key Terms 903

24 ★ The Texas Executive Branch *904*

The Governor 907
Qualifications *909*
Election and Term of Office *909*
Campaigns *910*
Removal of a Governor *911*
Succession *911*
Compensation *912*
Staff *912*
Executive Powers of the Governor *913*
Legislative Powers of the Governor *915*
Judicial Powers of the Governor *917*
The Office and Its Occupants *917*
The Plural Executive 917
Secretary of State *919*
Lieutenant Governor *919*
Attorney General *922*

Commissioner of the General Land Office   *922*
Commissioner of Agriculture   *923*
Comptroller of Public Accounts   *923*
Accountability of the Plural Executive   *924*
The Plural Executive and the Governor   *924*
Boards, Commissions, and Regulatory Agencies   925
Multimember Appointed Boards   *925*
Appointed Single Executives   *927*
Multimember Elected Boards   *928*
Making Agencies Accountable   *930*
Conclusion: Democracy and the Executive in Texas   931
Recommended Web Sites   932
Study Outline   932
Practice Quiz   933
Key Terms   933

25 ★ The Texas Judiciary   934

Court Structure   937
The Legal Process   941
How Judges Are Selected   944
Initial Appointment of Judges by the Governor   *945*
The Elections Become Really Partisan   *945*
The Name Game   *948*
Minority Representation in the Texas Judiciary   *949*
Alternative Means of Selection   *952*
The Importance of the Texas Courts   955
The Death Penalty   *955*
Other Criminal Punishments   *957*
The Integrity of the Texas Criminal Justice System   *958*
Civil Cases   *960*
Summary   962
Recommended Web Sites   962
Study Outline   963
Practice Quiz   964
Key Terms   964

26 ★ Local Government in Texas   966

County Government in Texas   969
Numerous County Offices: Checks and Balances or Built-In Problems?   *970*
Are Some Counties Too Small?   *972*
The Functions of County Government   *974*
County Governments in Perspective   *976*
City Government in Texas   977
Forms of Government in Texas Cities   *978*
A Tale of Three Cities   *980*
Special Districts   982
Types of Special Districts   *983*

School Districts *983*
Nonschool Special Districts *983*
Councils of Government (COGs) *988*
Summary 988
Recommended Web Sites 989
Study Outline 989
Practice Quiz 990
Key Terms 991

27 ★ Public Policy in Texas 992

Taxing and Spending in Texas 995
The Constitution and the Budget *996*
The Budgetary Process *997*
Revenue in Texas *998*
The Question of the Income Tax in Texas *1001*
Other State Revenue *1002*
Expenditures in Texas *1004*
The 2004 Budget Crisis in Texas *1004*
Crime and Corrections Policy 1006
History of the Prison System *1006*
Texas Crime and Corrections *1007*
Education Policy in Texas 1010
Desegregation *1012*
Equity in the Public School System *1012*
Educational Excellence and Accountability in Texas *1016*
Education Policy in Perspective *1018*
Welfare Policy 1018
Poverty in Texas *1018*
Welfare in Texas, 1935–96 *1020*
The Idea of Dependency and Welfare Reform *1022*
Evaluating Welfare Reform *1024*
Conclusion 1025
Recommended Web Sites 1025
Study Outline 1026
Practice Quiz 1027
Key Terms 1028

APPENDIX   *A1*
The Declaration of Independence   *A1*
The Articles of Confederation   *A4*
The Constitution of the United States of America   *A8*
Amendments to the Constitution   *A14*
The Federalist Papers   *A20*
Presidents and Vice Presidents   *A25*

GLOSSARY   *A27*

ENDNOTES   *A41*

ANSWER KEY   *A77*

PHOTO CREDITS   *A79*

INDEX   *A81*

This book has been and continues to be dedicated to developing a satisfactory response to the question more and more Americans are asking: Why should we be engaged with government and politics? Through the first six editions, we sought to answer this question by making the text directly relevant to the lives of the students who would be reading it. As a result, we tried to make politics interesting by demonstrating that students' interests are at stake and that they therefore need to take a personal, even selfish, interest in the outcomes of government. At the same time, we realized that students needed guidance in how to become politically engaged. Beyond providing students with a core of political knowledge, we needed to show them how they could apply that knowledge as participants in the political process. The "Get Involved" sections in each chapter help achieve that goal.

As events from the last several years have reminded us, "what government does" can be a matter of life and death. Recent events have reinforced the centrality of government in citizens' lives. The U.S. government has fought a war abroad, while claiming sweeping new powers at home that could compromise the liberties of its citizens. America's role in the world is discussed daily both inside and outside the classroom. Moreover, students and younger Americans have become more aware of and involved in politics, as the 2008 elections illustrated. Reflecting all of these trends, this new Seventh Edition shows more than any other book on the market (1) how students are connected to government; (2) how American government is connected to the world; and (3) why students should think critically about government and politics. These themes are incorporated in the following ways:

> **New "Get Involved" units show students how they can make a difference in politics.**　The 2008 elections produced a surge in political participation among young Americans, as well as changes in the ways that they participated. These full-page boxes use contemporary examples to explain how young people (even those with busy lives!) can get involved in politics. Specific, step-by-step instructions guide students through a range of possible political activities related to each chapter's topic. These new boxes replace the "Get Involved" sections that appeared as part of the chapter text in the Sixth Edition and have been rewritten to take account of the Internet's growing prominence as an avenue for political participation.

> **"Politics and Popular Culture" boxes connect politics to topics students are interested in.**　In each chapter "Politics and Popular Culture" boxes ask students to look critically at how politics intersects with television, film, music, cartoons, and the Internet. Drawing on a range of social science research, these boxes engage students in questions such as "Do non-news TV shows that include political content, like *The Daily Show with Jon Stewart*, have an effect on political knowledge?" "Is there a culture war?" and "Why do candidates sometimes prefer to be interviewed on talk shows rather than traditional news programs?"

› **Chapter introductions focus on "What Government Does and Why It Matters."** In recent decades, cynicism about "big government" has dominated the political zeitgeist. But critics of government often forget that governments do a great deal for citizens. Every year, Americans are the beneficiaries of billions of dollars of goods and services from government programs. Government "does" a lot, and what it does matters a great deal to everyone, including college students. At the start of each chapter, this theme is introduced and applied to the chapter's topic. The goal is to show students that government and politics mean something to their daily lives.

› **"America in the World" boxes show students how American government is connected to the world.** These one-page boxes in every chapter illustrate the important political role the United States plays abroad. Topics include "Should America Export Democracy?" "The American Constitution: A Model for the World?" "Participation and Democracy in Iraq," and "What Is Congress's Role in Foreign Policy?" These boxes exemplify the critical-analytical approach that characterizes the text and include "For Critical Analysis" questions.

› **"For Critical Analysis" questions are incorporated throughout the text.** "For Critical Analysis" questions in the margins of every chapter prompt students' own critical thinking about the material in the chapter, encouraging them to engage with the topic. The two "For Critical Analysis" questions that conclude each "America in the World" box get students to think more deeply about America's role in the world. The questions at the end of each "Politics and Popular Culture" box ask students to think critically about the intersection of politics and mass media. And the questions that follow the discussions of contending perspectives in each "Policy Debate" box invite students to reconsider their own perspective on the issue.

› **New "Politics Today" questions highlight discussions of current issues and recent events.** We believe that students value what they learn in the course more if they see how the course material relates to the issues and events in today's headlines. This Seventh Edition has been extensively updated with new sections on major events like the 2008 elections and the government's response to the recent housing and financial crisis, as well as contemporary examples throughout. New "Politics Today" questions in the margins of each chapter draw students' attention to discussions of recent events and ask questions to get them thinking critically about contemporary issues and events.

We continue to hope that our book will itself be accepted as a form of enlightened political action. This Seventh Edition is another chance. It is an advancement toward our goal. We promise to keep trying.

ACKNOWLEDGMENTS

Our students at Cornell, Johns Hopkins, Harvard, and Berkeley have been an essential factor in the writing and revising of this book. They have been our most immediate intellectual community, a hospitable one indeed. Another part of our community, perhaps a large suburb, is the discipline of political science itself. Our debt to the scholarship of our colleagues is scientifically measurable, probably to several decimal points, in the endnotes of each chapter. Despite many complaints that the field is too scientific or not scientific enough, political science is alive and well in the United States. It is an aspect of democracy itself, and it has grown and changed in response to the developments in government and politics that we have chronicled in our book. If we did a "time line" on the history of political science, it would show a close association with developments in "the American state." Sometimes the discipline has been out of phase and critical; at other times, it has been in phase and perhaps apologetic. But political science has never been at a loss for relevant literature, and without it, our job would have been impossible.

We are especially pleased to acknowledge our debt to the many colleagues who had a direct and active role in criticism and preparation of the manuscript. Our thanks go to:

FIRST EDITION REVIEWERS

Sarah Binder, Brookings Institution
Kathleen Gille, Office of Representative David Bonior
Rodney Hero, University of Colorado at Boulder
Robert Katzmann, Brookings Institution
Kathleen Knight, University of Houston
Robin Kolodny, Temple University
Nancy Kral, Tomball College
Robert C. Lieberman, Columbia University
David A. Marcum, University of Wyoming
Laura R. Winsky Mattei, State University of New York at Buffalo
Marilyn S. Mertens, Midwestern State University
Barbara Suhay, Henry Ford Community College
Carolyn Wong, Stanford University
Julian Zelizer, State University of New York at Albany

SECOND EDITION REVIEWERS

Lydia Andrade, University of North Texas
John Coleman, University of Wisconsin at Madison
Daphne Eastman, Odessa College
Otto Feinstein, Wayne State University
Elizabeth Flores, Delmar College
James Gimpel, University of Maryland at College Park
Jill Glaathar, Southwest Missouri State University

Shaun Herness, University of Florida
William Lyons, University of Tennessee at Knoxville
Andrew Polsky, Hunter College, City University of
    New York
Grant Reeher, Syracuse University
Richard Rich, Virginia Polytechnic
Bartholomew Sparrow, University of Texas at Austin

THIRD EDITION REVIEWERS

Bruce R. Drury, Lamar University
Andrew I. E. Ewoh, Prairie View A&M University
Amy Jasperson, University of Texas at San Antonio
Loch Johnson, University of Georgia
Mark Kann, University of Southern California
Robert L. Perry, University of Texas of the Permian
    Basin
Wayne Pryor, Brazosport College
Elizabeth A. Rexford, Wharton County Junior College
Andrea Simpson, University of Washington
Brian Smentkowski, Southeast Missouri State
    University
Nelson Wikstrom, Virginia Commonwealth University

FOURTH EDITION REVIEWERS

M. E. Banks, Virginia Commonwealth University
Lynn Brink, North Lake College
Mark Cichock, University of Texas at Arlington
Del Fields, St. Petersburg College
Nancy Kinney, Washtenaw Community College
William Klein, St. Petersburg College
Dana Morales, Montgomery College
Christopher Muste, Louisiana State University
Larry Norris, South Plains College
David Rankin, State University of New York at
    Fredonia
Paul Roesler, St. Charles Community College
J. Philip Rogers, San Antonio College
Greg Shaw, Illinois Wesleyan University
Tracy Skopek, Stephen F. Austin State University
Don Smith, University of North Texas
Terri Wright, Cal State, Fullerton

FIFTH EDITION REVIEWERS

Annie Benifield, Tomball College
Denise Dutton, Southwest Missouri State University
Rick Kurtz, Central Michigan University
Kelly McDaniel, Three Rivers Community College

Eric Plutzer, Pennsylvania State University
Daniel Smith, Northwest Missouri State University
Dara Strolovitch, University of Minnesota
Dennis Toombs, San Jacinto College–North
Stacy Ulbig, Southwest Missouri State University

SIXTH EDITION REVIEWERS

Janet Adamski, University of Mary Hardin-Baylor
Greg Andrews, St. Petersburg College
Louis Bolce, Baruch College
Darin Combs, Tulsa Community College
Sean Conroy, University of New Orleans
Paul Cooke, Cy Fair College
Vida Davoudi, Kingwood College
Robert DiClerico, West Virginia University
Corey Ditslear, University of North Texas
Kathy Dolan, University of Wisconsin, Milwaukee
Randy Glean, Midwestern State University
Nancy Kral, Tomball College
Mark Logas, Valencia Community College
Scott MacDougall, Diablo Valley College
David Mann, College of Charleston
Christopher Muste, University of Montana
Richard Pacelle, Georgia Southern University
Sarah Poggione, Florida International University
Richard Rich, Virginia Tech
Thomas Schmeling, Rhode Island College
Scott Spitzer, California State University–Fullerton
Dennis Toombs, San Jacinto College–North
John Vento, Antelope Valley College
Robert Wood, University of North Dakota

SEVENTH EDITION REVIEWERS

Molly Andolina, DePaul University
Nancy Bednar, Antelope Valley College
Paul Blakelock, Kingwood College
Amy Brandon, San Jacinto College
Jim Cauthen, John Jay College
Kevin Davis, North Central Texas College
Louis DeSipio, University of California–Irvine
Brandon Franke, Blinn College
Steve Garrison, Midwestern State University
Joseph Howard, University of Central Arkansas
Aaron Knight, Houston Community College
Paul Labedz, Valencia Community College
Elise Langan, John Jay College
Mark Logas, Valencia Community College
Eric Miller, Blinn College

Anthony O'Regan, Los Angeles Valley College
David Putz, Kingwood College
Chis Soper, Pepperdine University
Kevin Wagner, Florida Atlantic University
Laura Wood, Tarrant County College

We owe special thanks to John Forshee of San Jacinto College, who worked with us as a coauthor on earlier Texas editions. We are grateful for his important contributions to the material on Texas government and politics in this book, and for his valuable input on the online resources that accompany the Texas chapters.

We also must pay thanks to the other collaborators we have had on this project: Robert J. Spitzer of the State University of New York at Cortland; Mark Kann and Marcella Marlowe of the University of Southern California; and, most recently, Molly Andolina of DePaul University and Krista Jenkins of Fairleigh Dickinson University, who together contributed the new "Get Involved" boxes.

We are also grateful for the talents and hard work of several research assistants, whose contributions can never be adequately compensated. In particular, for his work on this Seventh Edition, we thank Kevin Wallsten.

We would like to give special thanks to Jacqueline Pastore at Cornell University, who not only prepared portions of the manuscript but also helped to hold the entire project together. We especially thank her for her hard work and dedication.

Perhaps above all, we wish to thank those at W. W. Norton. For its first five editions, editor Steve Dunn helped us shape the book in countless ways. Our current editor, Ann Shin, has carried on the Norton tradition of splendid editorial work. We thank Kelly Mitchell, Patty

Cateura, Elyse Rieder, and Rae Grant for devoting an enormous amount of time to finding new photos. For our student Web site and other media resources for the book, Dan Jost has been an energetic and visionary editor. Barbara Curialle copyedited the manuscript with Marian Johnson's superb direction, and project editor Carla Talmadge devoted countless hours keeping on top of myriad details. Ben Reynolds has been dedicated in managing production. Finally, we wish to thank Roby Harrington, the head of Norton's college department.

We are more than happy, however, to absolve all these contributors from any flaws, errors, and misjudgments that will inevitably be discovered. We wish the book could be free of all production errors, grammatical errors, misspellings, misquotes, missed citations, etc. From that standpoint, a book ought to try to be perfect. But substantively we have not tried to write a flawless book; we have not tried to write a book to please everyone. We have again tried to write an effective book, a book that cannot be taken lightly. Our goal was not to make every reader a political scientist or a political activist. Our goal was to restore politics as a subject matter of vigorous and enjoyable discourse, recapturing it from the bondage of the thirty-second sound bite and the thirty-page technical briefing. Every person can be knowledgeable because everything about politics is accessible. One does not have to be a television anchorperson to profit from political events. One does not have to be a philosopher to argue about the requisites of democracy, a lawyer to dispute constitutional interpretations, an economist to debate a public policy. We would be very proud if our book contributes in a small way to the restoration of the ancient art of political controversy.

BENJAMIN GINSBERG
THEODORE J. LOWI
MARGARET WEIR
ANTHONY CHAMPAGNE
EDWARD J. HARPHAM

November 2008

SEVENTH TEXAS EDITION

We the People

AN INTRODUCTION TO AMERICAN POLITICS